# Shifting Suburbs
## Reinventing Infrastructure for Compact Development

## About ULI

The mission of the Urban Land Institute is to provide leadership in the responsible use of land and in creating and sustaining thriving communities worldwide. ULI is committed to

- Bringing together leaders from across the fields of real estate and land use policy to exchange best practices and serve community needs;
- Fostering collaboration within and beyond ULI's membership through mentoring, dialogue, and problem solving;
- Exploring issues of urbanization, conservation, regeneration, land use, capital formation, and sustainable development;
- Advancing land use policies and design practices that respect the uniqueness of both the built and natural environments;
- Sharing knowledge through education, applied research, publishing, and electronic media; and
- Sustaining a diverse global network of local practice and advisory efforts that address current and future challenges.

Established in 1936, the Institute today has nearly 30,000 members worldwide, representing the entire spectrum of the land use and development disciplines. ULI relies heavily on the experience of its members. It is through member involvement and information resources that ULI has been able to set standards of excellence in development practice. The Institute has long been recognized as one of the world's most respected and widely quoted sources of objective information on urban planning, growth, and development.

## Abbreviations and Acronyms

| | | | |
|---|---|---|---|
| BAT | business access and transit | LRT | light-rail transit |
| BRT | bus rapid transit | SR | State Road |
| CoO | Corridors of Opportunity | TIF | tax increment financing |
| DART | Dallas Area Rapid Transit | TOD | transit-oriented development |

Recommended bibliographical listing:

Urban Land Institute. *Shifting Suburbs: Reinventing Infrastructure for Compact Development*. Washington, D.C.: Urban Land Institute, 2012.

ISBN: 978-0-87420-254-0

# About the ULI Infrastructure Initiative

The mission of the ULI Infrastructure Initiative is to promote more sustainable infrastructure investment choices and to foster an improved understanding of the links between infrastructure and land use. Because infrastructure is the foundation for metropolitan prosperity, and because it provides the physical framework for real estate investment, ULI has identified infrastructure as a key priority.

Established in 2007, the Initiative achieves its mission through a multifaceted program of work that leverages ULI's extensive public and private networks and includes research and education, publications, and convenings.

ULI's Infrastructure Initiative is led by full-time staff with a deep understanding of global infrastructure challenges and opportunities. An advisory group composed of industry leaders guides the program. Key ULI Infrastructure Initiative activities include

- A global infrastructure report, produced in collaboration with Ernst & Young since 2007;
- Ongoing programming to promote regional infrastructure solutions;
- Regular e-mail updates to infrastructure audiences; and
- Exploration of infrastructure topics relevant to ULI members and to ULI's public and private partners.

## About This Report

This report is part of a series of activities exploring suburban infrastructure opportunities and challenges. It includes observations from experts and leaders who participated in two forums held in Atlanta, Georgia, and Minneapolis, Minnesota, investigating how to plan and build infrastructure for compact development in the suburbs, along with other research and analysis by the ULI Infrastructure Initiative.

This work stream explores

- How public and private sector stakeholders are working together to build and retrofit suburban places;
- How infrastructure—including roads, transit, and more—can be transformed and leveraged to support compact development;
- How local governments and regional coalitions can position themselves for compact growth; and
- What funding, financing, and regulatory sources and tools are being used or are needed.

## Connect with the ULI Infrastructure Initiative

Visit the ULI Infrastructure Initiative's website (http://www.uli.org/infrastructure) to learn more about our work, and visit our blog (http://www.uli.org/infrastructureblog) to read about news and research of interest to the ULI network. Follow us on Twitter (@uli_infra). E-mail us to subscribe to our regular e-newsletter (infrastructure@uli.org).

We welcome new partners and sponsors. Contact us to explore opportunities to work with us (infrastructure@uli.org).

## Acknowledgments

The ULI Infrastructure Initiative gratefully acknowledges the Rockefeller Foundation for its support of this report and related activities. We also extend our thanks to ULI Atlanta and ULI Minnesota for hosting programs exploring this topic, to the speakers and attendees who participated, and to the many contributors to this report.

## ULI Senior Executives

**Patrick Phillips**
Chief Executive Officer

**Cheryl Cummins**
Executive Officer

**Michael Terseck**
Chief Financial Officer/Chief
   Administrative Officer

**Richard M. Rosan**
President, ULI Foundation

**Joe Montgomery**
Chief Executive, Europe

**David Howard**
Executive Vice President, Development
   and ULI Foundation

**Kathleen B. Carey**
Executive Vice President/Chief Content
   Officer

**Lela Agnew**
Executive Vice President,
   Communications

**Marilee Utter**
Executive Vice President, District
   Councils

## ULI Project Staff

**Rachel MacCleery**
Vice President, ULI Infrastructure Initiative

**Sarah Jo Peterson**
Research Director, ULI Infrastructure
   Initiative

**Casey Peterson**
Researcher, ULI Infrastructure Initiative

**James Mulligan**
Managing Editor

**Joanne Platt, Publications
Professionals LLC**
Manuscript Editor

**Betsy VanBuskirk**
Creative Director

**Deanna Pineda, Muse Advertising
Design**
Graphic Designer

**Craig Chapman**
Senior Director, Publishing Operations

## Authors

**Rachel MacCleery**
Vice President, ULI Infrastructure Initiative

**Casey Peterson**
Researcher, ULI Infrastructure Initiative

**Julie D. Stern**
JDS Communications

# Contents

# **Part I.** Introduction

In this report, the terms *suburb* and *suburban* can refer to a place's political or geographic location, but, more important, they reference its development form. The suburban places explored in this report's case studies began as spread-out, automobile-oriented areas. Suburban places can be found everywhere, including within city boundaries.

America's metropolitan areas have always been the scenes of dynamic change. In the great metropolitan dance, suburbs and central cities have each played starring roles in their turn, learning from each other, sharing missteps, collaborating, and competing.

Until World War II, most metropolitan action happened in cities, which served as retail, cultural, and workplace hubs. The suburbs were the boomtowns of the second half of the last century, the repositories of the post–World War II American dream, where ample space and strong consumer appetites combined to generate an unparalleled prosperity. During that period, central cities struggled, their economies and populations sapped by the suburban exodus and a host of political and policy failures.

The 1990s and early 21st century were a time of continued transformation for cities and suburbs alike. Many cities engineered remarkable economic turnarounds, employing a host of new tools to attract both private investment and people. Suburbs were changing as well. Some continued to thrive, but challenges mounted too. Inner suburbs struggled to update their image, infrastructure, and economic dynamism, whereas some outer

State Road 7 in Florida, before and after improvements. Investments in bus stop infrastructure have made waiting for the bus more comfortable for passengers. (STATE ROAD 7 COLLABORATIVE)

suburbs faced a wave of foreclosures and the terrible convergence of personal and civic financial crises.

At the same time, driven in part by powerful demographic forces, market preferences have been shifting. Signs point to an increasing appetite—especially among generation Y—for higher-density living patterns and for transportation options that include transit, walking, and biking.

Over the last two decades, driven in part by a desire to attract and retain a young talented workforce, suburban places have launched important initiatives aimed at meeting shifting market demands. Across the country, dozens, if not hundreds, of suburban places have worked to reimagine their future and to build or rebuild in more compact and sustainable ways.

The signs point to continued change—and a continued need for innovation—in the suburbs. The aging of the baby boomers—an upwardly mobile generation that helped fuel decades of suburban growth—means that one engine of suburban expansion is receding. According to the Brookings Institution, the suburbs are now home to a greater proportion of people age 45 and older than are cities, as the baby boom generation ages in place. In 2010, for the first time, the majority of the nation's poor lived in suburbs, as suburbs absorbed more of the national rise in metropolitan poverty. Immigrants also make up an increasingly important component of the suburban population.

The way that the U.S. Census Bureau aggregates population and economic data at the regional level can make it challenging to quantify what is happening in suburban places, and to compare that information with growth patterns in cities. But clearly, efforts at suburban redevelopment and reinvention are continuing and will likely accelerate in the years to come. As this transformation continues, infrastructure is and will be a key piece of the compact suburban growth puzzle.

## Infrastructure for a More Compact, Walkable Future in the Suburbs

As American suburbs build in more compact ways—with higher-density development clustered in nodes or along corridors and with increasing options for getting around without a car—reworking or rethinking infrastructure can be essential. For compact development to occur, developers and municipalities must determine how to plan, fund, and finance the often costly and complicated infrastructure required for suburban compact growth. That infrastructure can include transit investments, structured parking, intricate street grids, sidewalks, streetlighting, and water, sewer, and other utility upgrades.

*The case studies in this report illuminate the infrastructure side of the suburban compact development story.*

A rich body of work, undertaken by ULI and other organizations, explores what works and what does not work in suburban redevelopment, what is happening nationwide, and where American suburbs are heading. This report complements that work by providing case studies that highlight the infrastructure aspects of eight redevelopment efforts from across the country.

The report looks at infrastructure in the context of the development project. It examines the infrastructure that was built and how that infrastructure was paid for, in an effort to illuminate the shape that infrastructure investments are taking and the tools being used to fund and finance them.

Before upgrades were made along the Aurora Corridor in Shoreline, Washington, buses obstructed traffic in order to pick up passengers waiting without shelters. (CITY OF SHORELINE)

## Suburban Development Types

The case studies explored in this report represent five overlapping compact and walkable suburban development or redevelopment types:

- **Suburban mall retrofits.** Built on the site of dying or obsolete shopping malls, these projects transform sprawling parking lots and mall complexes into compact, mixed-use places. These projects take advantage of consolidated landownership patterns and a sophisticated set of financing and regulatory tools. Examples included in this report are Belmar, Colorado, and CityCentre in Houston, Texas.

- **Suburban transit-oriented development.** Many transit-oriented development (TOD) opportunities are located in the suburbs. These projects seek to leverage their location near fixed-rail transit stations or bus transit corridors to build in higher-density ways, connecting the development with transit using sidewalks, bikeways, and other kinds of transportation infrastructure. Examples included in this report are projects in Richardson, Texas.

- **Suburban arterials or commercial corridors.** These efforts seek to transform aging or dysfunctional land uses and transportation infrastructure along highly traveled stretches of road. Such endeavors often focus on the densification of identified nodes and involve investments in transit service, especially bus transit. Examples in this report include State Road 7 in Florida and the Aurora Corridor project in Shoreline, Washington. As described in more detail below, this type is proving to be one of the most challenging forms of suburban redevelopment.

- **Wholesale or large-scale suburban transformation.** By their very nature, such transformations are rare. The redevelopment of Tysons Corner in Fairfax, Virginia—now simply called Tysons—is an example of an effort to reshape in a fundamental way how a suburban place functions. Tysons has been explored extensively elsewhere and is not included in this report. This report examines how Dublin, Ohio, is attempting to launch a similar transformation. These efforts require strong leadership and support from regional and local planning bodies, including metropolitan planning organizations.

Improvements along the Aurora Corridor have included a new pedestrian bridge, landscaped medians, and upgrades to utility infrastructure.
(HDR ENGINEERING INC.)

■ **Suburban town centers.** Suburban town centers are being developed or enhanced in many communities across the country. These mixed-use hubs offer many of the options that a larger city might provide—entertainment, residential buildings, offices— but in a suburban or small-town setting. Many suburban town centers are being retrofitted on existing sites—Belmar, Colorado, is an example explored in this report— but they can also be built on greenfield sites.

These typologies are not mutually exclusive; a suburban TOD might be built on the site of an obsolete suburban mall, for example. And additional typologies likely exist. These descriptions are offered as a helpful way of thinking about the compact suburban development projects that are happening across the country.

## Two Key Challenges and Opportunities

Over the last few decades, much progress has been made, and many lessons have been learned, in the art and science of the redevelopment of suburban sites. Looking both at the projects examined in this report and beyond them, two important overlapping challenges and opportunities emerge. The rebirth of suburban arterials and the reimaging of inner-ring suburbs for more compact growth will be essential components of efforts to create a new kind of suburban future.

### Suburban Arterials

Across the country, approaches to suburban arterials and commercial corridors remain works in progress. Designed for easy access by car to retail destinations, or for the swift movement of through-traffic, many of these corridors are disjointed jumbles of strip retail centers, utility wires, narrow or nonexistent sidewalks, parking lots, and extensive curb cuts. You get the picture.

For these places, it can be hard to imagine an alternate future, to say nothing of actually building one. Because of their important transportation role, and because of the development challenges they pose, they are often overlooked or disregarded as priorities for redevelopment. And even when a vision is in place, coordination across multiple jurisdictions, land assembly, prioritization of development nodes and sites (often necessary because of the sheer volume of land involved), and infrastructure investment needs all pose challenges—challenges that public and private stakeholders are still developing tools to effectively address.

But commercial corridors and suburban arterials represent an important opportunity. Despite being home to extensive amounts of large, underused and low-value land, they are often the sites of important commercial, retail, and entertainment activities in suburban locales. And despite their infrastructure challenges, they often have preexisting transit service, especially bus service, that can be leveraged with targeted investments like improved bus facilities and enhanced bus frequency.

How to make progress in unlocking the redevelopment potential of these corridors is an area that deserves additional attention.

## First-Ring Suburbs

First-ring suburbs are another area of opportunity. "America's first-ring suburbs," noted ULI's CEO Patrick Phillips, "could be the sweet spot for future growth." In many cases, these suburbs are already well served by transit, roads, and other transportation infrastructure, including highways, and they were designed in an efficient, adaptable urban pattern. They are home to well-established neighborhoods with mature trees and other amenities and have the locational advantage of being close to the center of a metropolitan region and to other suburbs. All of these features make inner suburbs attractive places for redevelopment.

However, redevelopment in first-ring suburbs can be a challenge. Convincing residents of the need for change can be difficult; local government bodies don't always sing from the same song book; and—importantly—modifying and upgrading the often outmoded infrastructure that would make redevelopment feasible or attractive can be challenging and expensive. In some cases, readily available redevelopment sites are not obvious. Still, solving the redevelopment challenge in first-ring suburbs is an effort worth taking seriously.

## Thinking on a Broader Scale

Stepping back and looking at a broader, metropolitan-level scale, the implications of changing demographics and preferences on regional transportation investment priorities could clearly be profound; more compact growth trajectories could require significant shifts in the types of transportation improvements that will be needed in the coming years.

Metropolitan planning organizations have a critical role to play in understanding and anticipating demographic and market shifts, and in ensuring the most strategic use of increasingly scarce public transportation dollars. To the extent that metropolitan planning organizations can help foster consensus around the need to use transportation investments to help advance more compact forms of suburban development, they will be key partners in the suburban redevelopment effort.

Houston's CityCentre project, which replaced an obsolete mall, emphasizes pedestrian-friendly features and green space. (CITYCENTRE)

As the portal to critical transportation resources, state and local departments of transportation are other key stakeholders. These agencies can help support compact development by building or rebuilding multimodal, human-scale streets, prioritizing investments in transit and transit-supportive infrastructure, modifying parking requirements, and taking other related actions.

## The Infrastructure Piece of the Puzzle

The U.S. population is expected to grow by another 95 million people over the next 30 years, making the United States one of the fastest-growing countries in the world. The vast majority of that growth will take place in metropolitan areas, and as has been the case in the last 40 years, the majority of metropolitan growth will likely occur outside the central core, in suburban places.

Although the story of compact suburban development and redevelopment is not a new one, it is one that is acquiring new energy. The good news is that the momentum is shifting away from sprawling, auto-oriented growth patterns in many places. The bad news is that changing the way development happens, and putting the appropriate infrastructure and other policies in place, are still a formidable task—despite the experience that the country is accumulating.

Compact development in the suburbs often requires extensive cross-jurisdictional infrastructure planning and coordination, as well as the commitment of many different players, including sometimes-overlapping local government entities, state departments of transportation, developers, and others.

To ensure that today's suburbs become more compact, sustainable places for the future, stakeholders will need to work together to identify and implement innovative solutions to infrastructure coordination, funding, and financing challenges.

Despite the progress made and lessons learned, these efforts are challenging, and there is still work to be done. We hope that the case studies and lessons learned in this report will shed light on the infrastructure piece of the suburban development and redevelopment puzzle and will help inform continued efforts to develop more compact and walkable places in the suburbs.

# Part II. Lessons Learned

The projects explored in part III of this report are works in progress. They run the gamut from suburban mall retrofits and arterial or corridor reinventions to comprehensive rethinking of development patterns for a whole town. Each project offers its own food for thought, and in looking at this set of projects as a whole, themes emerge.

Key elements have been distilled here, providing insights into two basic questions: What successful strategies have been employed to make progress toward building more compact, pedestrian-friendly places? and What are the stumbling blocks that are obstructing additional progress?

Some of these elements are focused squarely on infrastructure, and some have broader implications.

This rendering shows plans for the transformation of automobile-centric Rockville Pike in Montgomery County, Maryland, into a walkable, transit-oriented corridor with center-running bus rapid transit. (FEDERAL REALTY INVESTMENT TRUST)

# Winning Strategies

*What successful strategies have been employed to progress toward building more compact, pedestrian-friendly places?*

**Partnerships.** Effective partnerships are at the core of many of the efforts to transform the suburban places explored in this report, with public and private sector partnerships long recognized as essential. The West End project in Minnesota demonstrates the value of long-term public and private collaboration. Partnerships among private sector actors are also emerging as powerful organizing forces. In Montgomery County, Maryland, the White Flint Partnership is aggregating the resources of key real estate players to collectively address infrastructure challenges.

**A comprehensive approach to infrastructure and access.** Stakeholders from many or most of the places explored in this report have creatively and comprehensively considered the infrastructure and transportation needs of their projects. For the Belmar project in Lakewood, Colorado, an urban street grid was the transportation pattern of choice. Designers of Minnesota's West End project carefully orchestrated the reworking of utility infrastructure. And in the case of the Aurora Corridor in Shoreline, Washington, project leaders are seeking to make the most of bus system improvements with comprehensive upgrades to the corridor and public realm.

**Programming and place management.** If you build it, they will come. But will they come back? The projects explored in this report are using a variety of strategies to foster sustained engagement with customers and residents. Festivals, concerts, farmers markets, and other special events draw visitors and interest to the CityCentre project in Houston, as well as other projects in this report. Ongoing investment ensures a pleasant user experience. And organizational tools like business improvement districts and community improvement districts apply coordination and promotion methods, some developed for shopping mall or downtown contexts, to suburban places. These are the soft infrastructure strategies needed for success.

**Public space and plazas; trails and sidewalks.** Sidewalks and trails provide the connective tissue for compact suburban places, and public space and plazas can provide the heart. Much more than an afterthought, they are essential infrastructure elements. CityCentre Houston's central plaza is the gathering point for hundreds of events each year, and upgraded, 7.5-foot-wide (2.3 m) sidewalks and landscaped medians are providing pedestrian access along Washington's Aurora Corridor. Public realm investments are at the core of the efforts to reinvent the White Flint area in Maryland.

**Proactive planning.** Putting the planning pieces in place—market studies, infrastructure strategies, zoning changes—can help facilitate and attract compact growth. Whether the target for transformation is large scale or site specific, proactive planning can remove uncertainty, speeding redevelopment and ensuring that it happens according to a larger vision for the community. Dublin, Ohio, is an example of a place that is carefully laying the groundwork for more compact future development.

**Stakeholder engagement and buffering of existing neighborhoods.** Public involvement can help tame opposition to and build support for projects. Richardson, Texas, has built extensive public engagement into its transit-oriented development strategy, and the White Flint, Maryland, partners harnessed the power of social media to build public support for the corridor's transformation. A clear articulation of public benefits was essential. And a commitment to protecting existing neighborhoods from development impacts, including increased traffic, meant that a road in the West End project in Minnesota could not be extended.

*Above:* Mixed-use development makes for a more walkable experience at Belmar. (CITY OF LAKEWOOD) *Below:* The pedestrian bridge on the Aurora Corridor connects to the three-mile (4.8 km) Interurban Trail network. (CITY OF SHORELINE)

**Riding the demographic wave.** The localities examined in this report are working to capitalize on growing demand for compact, walkable places. Members of generation Y, America's largest single generation since the baby boomers, favor a more urban vibe. Dublin, Ohio, is an example of a place making a major mental and programmatic shift: it is retooling its sprawling suburban downtown to compete in a shifting marketplace and to attract companies that care greatly about where their workers (or potential workers) want to live. Dublin recognizes that it can ride the demographic wave, or risk missing it.

**Many sources of funding.** To build the transformative infrastructure required by these projects, many different sources of funding and a variety of financing tools were necessary. In the White Flint area of Maryland, special property assessments volunteered by the property owners are paying for a portion of the transportation costs. A nearly $2 million federal grant, along with assistance from a number of foundations, has helped State Route 7 stakeholders in Florida create a plan for the road. In Belmar, Colorado, the developer fronted the transportation construction costs and is slowly being repaid by the city. For these projects, no one-size funding approach would fit.

## Stumbling Blocks

*What are the stumbling blocks that are obstructing additional progress? And what are some potential avenues for change?*

**Trouble working across boundaries.** Compact development in the suburbs often requires extensive cross-jurisdictional planning and coordination, as well as the commitment of many different players, including sometimes-overlapping local government entities, state departments of transportation, developers, and others. Although both the Corridors of Opportunity project in Minneapolis–Saint Paul and the State Route 7 effort in Florida show how regions are striving to crack this nut, working across boundaries or jurisdictions remains a challenge just about everywhere.

Although not all suburban redevelopment projects cross political boundaries, many do. And even those that do not often rely on regional investments in transit, for example, or they can run into other regional challenges (in Shoreline, Washington, for example, corridor improvements end at the jurisdiction's southern border with Seattle).

Looking forward, the development and adoption of creative models for regional cooperation and investment will be an important component of efforts to redevelop the suburbs.

**Funding.** Although local leaders and developers have become adept at pulling together many sources of funding (see above), finding the resources to plan and build projects, and to make the infrastructure investments needed, remains a challenge. For every project built, there are likely many that were unable to proceed because of a lack of funding.

Looking forward, two funding opportunities are worthy of particular attention. The first is ensuring that *state transportation dollars* are going to transportation investments that support compact development in the suburbs. Building or rebuilding complete streets that meet the needs of all users, and making other investments that help lay the groundwork for redevelopment, are important priorities.

Houston's CityCentre project emphasizes high-quality design. (CITYCENTRE)

Public hearings and charrettes guided planning efforts by the State Road 7 Collaborative. (STATE ROAD 7 COLLABORATIVE)

The second is the opportunity to develop and use *more sustainable funding solutions* that capitalize on and reinforce the link between transportation—especially transit—and land use/real estate. These solutions include the use of value-capture mechanisms that leverage real estate or property values to pay for infrastructure, such as special assessment districts or tax increment financing (TIF).

**Skill sets.** Developing suburban areas into more compact, urban, walkable environments can require a new set of skills on the part of public entities and private sector developers alike. Traffic analyses can require new paradigms—for example, acceptance of higher levels of projected congestion or a willingness to dedicate a travel lane to transit. Often, zoning must be modified, new public/private partnerships must be crafted, new financing arrangements must be established, parking must be rethought, new designs must be created, and other shifts must be made in order for dense, mixed-use projects to be possible.

These paradigm shifts require deviations from business as usual, and sometimes a leap of faith on the part of the various parties involved. Looking forward, as compact suburban projects become more common, skill sets will become more developed. In the meantime, this area is an important opportunity for more learning and exchange.

**Entitlements and zoning.** Getting the approvals necessary to move forward with projects—even those that are widely supported by local leaders—can be time-consuming and expensive. Although approval processes are important mechanisms for protecting community values, they can add elements of uncertainty that cloud the future of suburban redevelopment.

Looking forward, improving the zoning and entitlement process to facilitate compact suburban development is an important effort that community leaders seeking this kind of development should consider taking on.

**Community resistance.** Community resistance to suburban development or redevelopment projects can slow them down, or kill them entirely. And fear of opposition can push development efforts away from suburban locations before they even get started. Winning over skeptical residents can appear a daunting task, but it is one worth making, and early and consistent stakeholder engagement is a critical component of suburban redevelopment efforts.

Looking ahead, social media will be an important tool—joining more traditional tools like community meetings—in winning support for redevelopment. A clear articulation of benefits, the creation of measures to ensure that existing single-family homes are buffered from development impacts (by stepping down heights or density, for example), and thoughtful integration of existing and new development, residents, and businesses can be other important components in the efforts to win community support.

# **Part III.** Infrastructure for a New Suburbia: Case Studies from Across America

# Dublin, Ohio, and the Bridge Street Corridor

*Dublin, a wealthy suburban community located 13 miles (21 km) northwest of downtown Columbus, has launched a bold effort to reimagine its core, located along the central axis of Bridge Street. Rather than continuing old patterns of growth, Dublin is positioning itself for a compact, walkable future.*

### Lessons from Dublin

■ Demographic shifts and enlightened self-interest create new opportunities for communities to position themselves for more compact and sustainable growth.

■ Companies making decisions about where to locate today are focused on where talented young workers want to be instead of—as in the past—where CEOs want to live.

■ Dublin's public leaders have proactively launched an overarching planning effort, rather than waiting to respond to specific development proposals.

Home to several corporate headquarters, Dublin has been one of the fastest-growing cities in the state, with its population increasing from only 300 in 1970 to around 40,000 in 2010. By most measures—fiscal health, resident satisfaction, levels of public service, quality-of-life indicators, and others—Dublin has been an extremely successful suburban community, riding the wave of forces that drove the suburbanization of development activity nationally over the last 40 years.

Recognizing that the forces shaping the next 40 years of development will likely be very different, Dublin has launched an ambitious plan to rethink and convert the 1,000-acre (405 ha) core of its community. Located along Bridge Street and bounded on the north by Interstate 270, this section of the city is slated for transformation from a low-density, automobile-dependent area into a dense, mixed-use, and pedestrian-friendly corridor composed of seven new districts, with new offices and compact residential buildings complementing a preserved historic downtown.

As city manager, Terry Foegler helped lead the plan to transform Dublin. Examining demographic trends, Foegler recognized that the market forces that had shaped Dublin over the last 40 years were shifting: Dublin needed to provide housing options for talented young professionals and other workers, in order to position itself to appeal to companies as a place where those workers want to live. Its aging baby boomers were also seeking different types of housing products and environments.

*Above:* Dublin's vision includes a pedestrian bridge connecting a park to the historic district across the Scioto River. (GOODY CLANCY/CITY OF DUBLIN, OHIO)

*Preceding page, clockwise from top left:* Developers of CityCentre inserted a street grid into what was formerly a mall; the Aurora Corridor provides a vital link into downtown Seattle; the State Road 7 Collaborative engaged local citizens in planning activities. (CITYCENTRE, HDR ENGINEERING INC., STATE ROAD 7 COLLABORATIVE)

This rendering, part of the Bridge Street Corridor Vision Plan, shows how Dublin is reimagining its future. (GOODY CLANCY/CITY OF DUBLIN, OHIO)

What emerged from the city's planning process was "a development idea radically different from anything Dublin has ever experienced," said Foegler. A new vision plan for the city was adopted in October 2010.

Market studies estimated that demand for office space and retail space will continue to be strong in Dublin over the next 20 years. City leaders are aiming to absorb as much of that growth as possible in the Bridge Street corridor, and they have modified zoning to accommodate it, shifting to form-based codes. Residential density could intensify from the city's current limit of five units per acre (12 units/ha) in its highest-density multifamily zone to 50, 60, or even 70 units per acre (125, 150, or 175 units/ha) within the corridor.

Integrating and leveraging the design and implementation of key infrastructure projects with the proposed private investments will be key to advancing Dublin's vision. The city's east–west corridor of Bridge Street is a busy state highway made up of four lanes

An aerial photo shows existing conditions in the Bridge Street corridor. (GOOGLE MAPS)

The Bridge Street Corridor Vision Plan is guiding the redevelopment of land uses in Dublin. (GOODY CLANCY/CITY OF DUBLIN, OHIO)

and a median. Working with the Ohio Department of Transportation, Dublin hopes to modify the street to accommodate potential future transit service and to make other improvements, including building wider sidewalks and green spaces. The city also has plans to add an extensive grid pattern of roadways, as well as connections bisecting the corridor, to provide alternatives to driving through the downtown historic district.

Dublin is now moving toward implementing the first elements of its 2010 vision plan. Detailed traffic and infrastructure impact studies have been conducted, and the city has drawn up transportation guidelines. Most recently, Dublin has completed fiscal impact and infrastructure modeling and has adopted a form-based zoning code. The city is exploring opportunities for using tax increment financing, special assessment districts,

This rendering shows improvements to the park and path system, with residential development located near green space. (GOODY CLANCY/CITY OF DUBLIN, OHIO)

and public/private partnerships to fund public infrastructure—including structured parking, new streets, and public spaces. Developers have responded with a number of high-density redevelopment project proposals that are currently under review by the city.

Dublin is approaching its economic transformation from a position of strength, anticipating future demographic shifts and modifying infrastructure and land use so that population and employment will continue to grow—and grow in more sustainable ways—in the coming decades. It is aiming to maintain a high quality of life while positioning itself to remain competitive within the context of future drivers of growth.

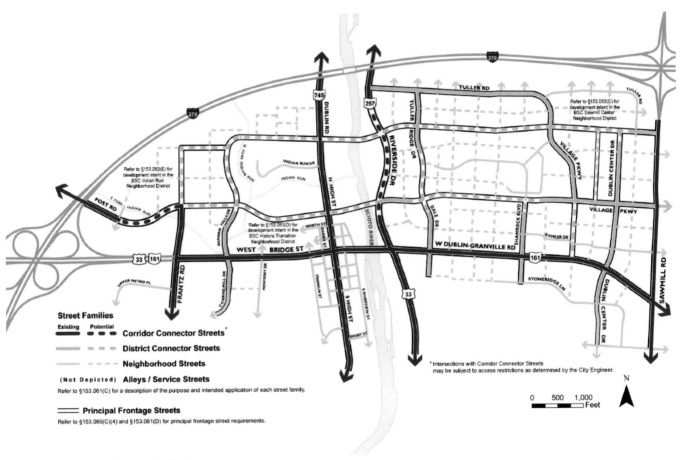

**Dublin is planning a new, dense network of streets.** (GOODY CLANCY/CITY OF DUBLIN, OHIO)

# Aurora Corridor, Shoreline, Washington

*The Aurora Corridor, an arterial in suburban Seattle, is making a suite of bold infrastructure investments. Investments in sidewalks, utility lines, and transportation infrastructure are helping the corridor position itself to take advantage of market trends and regional bus system upgrades.*

A new pedestrian bridge enhances connectivity along the Aurora Corridor in Shoreline. (CITY OF SHORELINE)

### Lessons from the Aurora Corridor

- Bus rapid transit can help foster the development of a horizontally mixed-use corridor and make possible a walkable lifestyle for those who live along it.

- Suburban arterials can be made more attractive, functional, and safe for automobiles and pedestrians alike.

Three miles (4.8 km) of State Road 99, referred to locally as Aurora Avenue North, run through Shoreline, a suburban community with a population of about 53,000 people that abuts Seattle's northern border. Before it was rebuilt, it had four travel lanes and one turn lane, and carried a large amount of through- and local traffic—40,000 vehicles and 7,000 bus riders used the corridor each day. The highly congested, complicated road was plagued by one of the highest accident rates in the state, with nearly one accident per day and one fatality per year. With few sidewalks or curbs, conditions on the corridor did not support walking or transit use.

Land uses within the corridor were part of the problem. Although the corridor is Shoreline's Main Street, housing about 90 percent of the city's taxable value, the community wanted to address the strip pattern of gas stations, shopping centers, convenience stores, and auto-oriented businesses, as well as "colorful" businesses like adult clubs and tobacco and alcohol stores.

An extensive planning and community involvement process was initiated in 1998. The City Council adopted a concept design in 1999 that called for improving safety, supporting increased transit, balancing local and regional movements, catalyzing economic growth, improving aesthetics, and preserving existing neighborhoods.

In 2005, the city of Shoreline began a comprehensive overhaul of the corridor. Infrastructure improvements on the majority of the corridor, from 145th to 192nd Street, are complete, and the project's first phase won a 2008 Award of Excellence for Best City Project from the Federal Highway Administration and the Washington State Department of Transportation. The right-of-way plan for the remaining streetscape from 192nd to 205th Street has been approved by the state of Washington, with construction scheduled for January 2013.

Construction is expected to be completed in 2014 and to cost about $120 million, with funding drawn from the city's capital improvement program and a mix of county, state, and federal dollars. The city has become adept at chasing external grants and funding to pay for the project; Shoreline taxpayers have covered only 10 percent of the project cost.

When completed, Aurora Avenue will feature landscaped medians, 7.5-foot (2.3 m) sidewalks on each side set four feet (1.2 m) back from the road, overhead utility lines relocated underground, new lighting, a north–south multimodal trail paralleling the road, and a public plaza to provide recreational and gathering space. Colored, scored concrete and artwork enhance crossings at intersections. The new corridor features two travel lanes in each direction. The original two-way center turn lane has been converted to a landscaped median with focused left-turn lanes and U-turn pockets.

In tandem with the transportation investments, the city upgraded utility infrastructure, including water, sewer, electricity, and communications conduits, at a cost of about $3,750 per frontage foot ($12,375/m). Unsightly power lines have been moved underground, and street lighting has been improved.

These investments are positioning Shoreline to take advantage of enhanced regional bus service that is expected in 2013, called RapidRide (see sidebar). Within Shoreline, bus reliability and travel times will be improved by the creation of new BAT (business access and transit) lanes, an innovation developed by the city, where right-hand lanes in each direction will be restricted to buses and right turns. "We invented the BAT term," said Kirk McKinley, transportation services manager for the city of Shoreline and project manager for the Aurora Corridor project, "because we had so much concern from the business community about walls of buses blocking views of their businesses. We

This map shows the three-mile (4.8 km) scope of the Aurora Corridor investments. (CITY OF SHORELINE)

These images show the Aurora Corridor before and after improvements, which included reconfiguration of traffic, creation of sidewalks and landscaped medians, installation of new lighting, and more. (CITY OF SHORELINE)

## RapidRide in King County, Washington

The Aurora Corridor project is seeking to take advantage of bus enhancements planned throughout King County, Washington. When the system is completed, the county will be home to 64 miles (103 km) of bus rapid transit service in semidedicated lanes.

Six high-usage bus corridors were chosen for significant upgrades in bus service, branded RapidRide. RapidRide's hybrid buses along the six lines arrive every ten minutes during peak periods and every 15 minutes during off-peak periods, and real-time displays at each station let passengers know when the next bus is coming. Other intelligent transportation system upgrades employed throughout the system include an off-board payment system and traffic signal prioritization for approaching buses.

Four of the six lines have been completed to date. The final two bus rapid transit lines, which will extend RapidRide service to the Aurora Corridor in Shoreline and to South King County, will be completed in September 2013. Complementary transportation investments in the road and pedestrian infrastructure are being made in selected locations throughout the system.

Funding for RapidRide is being drawn from a variety of local, state, and federal sources. At the local level, RapidRide has received $70 million in local capital investment, and a one-cent sales tax approved by King County voters in 2006 covers about 60 percent of the system's operating costs. Seattle's Bridging the Gap initiative, also passed in 2006, is helping fund road and traffic improvements that will enhance bus speed and service. RapidRide has also accumulated $120 million in state and federal grants, including $93 million from the Federal Transit Administration's Very Small Starts grant program. In November 2011, a $37.5 million federal grant was approved to fund the system's final two corridors.

decided to spin it around and call them 'business access' lanes, and that's been very helpful."

Dan Eernissee, economic development manager for the city of Shoreline and a former private sector developer, said that the investments are encouraging local landowners—many of whom are absentee landlords or trust funds—to redevelop their properties. "The city has to think like a developer," Eernissee advised, "to ask, 'What's going to catalyze the landowner to go out and find funds and invest in that property, to do something different?' You need to increase the spread between costs and rental income."

New bus stops, business access and transit lanes, and other improvements set the stage for regional RapidRide upgrades to come in 2013. (CITY OF SHORELINE)

As examples of how a city can reduce costs, Eernissee suggested lowering fees, changing zoning, speeding up the development approval process, and improving infrastructure. As examples of what cities can do to enable landowners to increase rents, Eernissee suggested place making—creating appealing locations where people want to live, work, and play—and reducing the cost of living by providing transit.

Eernissee also focused on what bus rapid transit (BRT) can offer. "With stops about a half mile [0.8 km] apart, the entire corridor—not just station areas—is activated. No one's going to ask, 'Do I live near a station?' Instead, they'll ask, 'Do I live on the line?' That's what we have to sell." The city staff projects that living along the BRT line will save motorists between $2,000 and $8,000 a year while connecting places along the line and system. The BRT line will allow for a horizontally mixed-use corridor, without the high costs and development expertise required to create a great vertical mixed-use development.

Although the corridor improvement project is not yet complete, the results have already been impressive, with accidents falling 60 percent and some redevelopment activity occurring—including a five-acre (2.0 ha) parcel that will include senior housing, market rate and affordable housing, and a new YMCA building. However, Shoreline faces challenges it can't control. Immediately south of Shoreline, State Road 99 remains unchanged, and the city of Seattle and Washington State Department of Transportation currently have no plans to upgrade the road.

*Facing page:* Infrastructure improvements have made the Aurora Corridor much more appealing. (CITY OF SHORELINE)

## Belmar, Lakewood, Colorado

*With a population of 144,000, Lakewood is Colorado's fifth-most-populous city. Located immediately west of Denver, the suburb is now home to Belmar, a mixed-use, compact, and sustainable urban-style center built on the site of the Villa Italia Mall.*

*Above:* Belmar's ice skating rink is an important amenity in the new community-oriented town center. (BELMAR, LAKEWOOD, COLORADO)

*Facing page:* Belmar features townhouses built in the American mercantile style. *Insets:* Belmar added new life to an obsolete shopping mall. (CITY OF LAKEWOOD)

### Lessons from Belmar

■ The urban-scale street grid is a classic choice.

■ Innovative financing arrangements can enable a private landowner to build infrastructure, with public reimbursements to follow.

■ The competitive advantage that compact, mixed-use development can have is demonstrated by Belmar.

Named after the former Belmar estate on which it sits, Belmar was designed to give Lakewood a downtown. The massive 103-acre (42 ha) site has been transformed into 3.3 million square feet (306,580 m²) of new development on 22 urban-scale blocks. Nearing complete buildout, Belmar now contains 880,000 square feet (81,755 m²) of retail space, 250,000 square feet (23,226 m²) of office space, 5,000 public parking spaces, 800 residential units (a mix of owner-occupied and rental housing), and two education institutions, as well as public plazas, art, and green space.

When it opened in the mid-1960s, the Villa Italia Mall—composed of 1.2 million square feet (111,484 m²) of mall space and surface parking lots—was one of the most productive regional malls west of the Mississippi River. For several decades, it was a vital member of the Lakewood community; at its peak in 1994, it generated $3.12 million in sales taxes. But by the late 1990s, occupancy had declined, storefronts were boarded up, and the property was in need of redevelopment. In 1997, city voters authorized the use of urban renewal powers.

Having to choose between building another mall and developing something entirely new, city officials decided to repurpose the massive site in a way that would achieve civic and economic goals. In 1998, the city formed a partnership with Denver-based Continuum Partners to redevelop the mall.

Building the right infrastructure has been a key consideration. After clearing the site and conducting environmental remediation in 2001, Continuum Partners designed a new grid-based street system, with a matrix of 22 streets scaled to the size of city blocks. The city assumed ownership of the streets after completion. Belmar features wide sidewalks and narrow roads, encouraging walking and slowing traffic. Over-the-road cable lighting creates atmosphere and a sense of intimacy. Parking is concentrated in three large public garages with a total of 3,000 spaces, in addition to roughly 2,000 street and surface spaces. When the Denver area's light-rail West Line, which will run east–west about two miles (3.2 km) north of Belmar, opens in 2013, existing bus service with increased frequency will connect it to Belmar.

The entire site was rezoned to launch a phased development process in which the purpose of the blocks could be determined over time. To date, 800 new housing units have been built, a mix of apartments, condominiums, townhomes, and zero-lot-line homes. In addition to being compact, the housing is constructed in the American mercantile style, reflecting Denver's architectural history. Retailers on the site include a

mix of national chains (including Target—designed in an innovative fashion, with ground-floor parking below second-story retail—Whole Foods, Nordstrom Rack, and Best Buy) and local businesses, some of which receive subsidized rents to withstand increases in rents. A number of civic and cultural spaces were also developed to encourage creative and cultural activity in the area. A movie theater and a bowling alley round out Belmar's retail offerings.

Open space is an important component of the development, making up nine acres (3.6 ha) of the site. An urban park and public plaza serve as Bellmar's center and social hub. A commitment to increasing energy efficiency and reducing emissions has resulted in several buildings being certified as LEED (Leadership in Energy and Environmental Design) structures. Belmar also has one of the country's largest solar panel systems, with 8,000 solar panels that generate 20 percent of the site's energy needs. Almost 88 percent of the materials used in construction by weight were recycled or reused from the former mall site.

Funded through a public/private partnership, the roughly $850 million Belmar project has been financed with a combination of government bonds, federal grants, and equity from Continuum. To date, $160 million has been spent on infrastructure improvements, $40 million of which was financed by developer equity. (The garages alone cost $35 million, or about $14,000 per space.)

The bonds for the project are backed primarily by a property tax increment pledge and the imposition of a 2.5 percent public improvement fee by the developer on retail sales. To offset the public improvement fee, the city has waived 2 percent of the 3 percent sales tax on the site. Using revenues from the public improvement fee and property tax increment, Continuum will be reimbursed for the public infrastructure by 2028, reported Larry Dorr, director of finance for the city of Lakewood.

Belmar has dramatically increased the walkability, diversity, and attractiveness of the area by providing Lakewood with the downtown it never had. People come to Belmar from a wider area, more often, and at many different times of day than they did when the mall was there. Programmed activities, including farmers markets, holiday happenings, and an annual Italian festival, are creating new traditions for Lakewood's residents.

Although sales figures at Belmar declined during the recent recession, they decreased less than sales did elsewhere, indicating the strength, durability, and appeal of Belmar's retail offerings. Residential activity has also been satisfactory. Future phases will include even more housing (the property is zoned for 2,000 units), as well as other uses—including, possibly, a hotel. "People ask me all the time, when will Belmar be finished?" said Dorr. "And I don't know—not only when it will be finished but what it might look like when it is. The market is going to drive that."

*Above and facing page:* Belmar shoppers take advantage of the site's wide sidewalks. (BELMAR, LAKEWOOD, COLORADO) *Facing page, insets:* The Villa Italia Mall was razed and redeveloped as the Belmar project, a mix of retail businesses, programmed open space, and housing. (CITY OF LAKEWOOD)

# State Road 7, Broward and Miami-Dade Counties, Florida

*A broad coalition of stake-holders has been working for more than a decade to reshape State Road 7, a north–south arterial highway in southeastern Florida, into a more multi-modal corridor with dense development at specific nodes.*

An improved public space along State Road 7 has received a strong reception. (STATE ROAD 7 COLLABORATIVE)

## Lessons from State Road 7

■ A consensus vision and a master plan can help organize the infrastructure and development efforts of multiple municipalities along commercial corridors.

■ Funding for collaborative efforts and infrastructure improvements can be drawn from federal, state, and local sources, as well as nonprofits and foundations.

State Road 7 (SR-7) is a north–south arterial highway that runs through southeastern Florida's Broward and Miami-Dade Counties. Also designated U.S. Highway 441 for most of its length, the arterial is used by several popular bus routes and is frequently congested. SR-7 is squeezed between two bodies of water—the Everglades and the Atlantic Ocean.

SR-7 is lined with commercial strip development built in the 1960s and 1970s—aging businesses that are having trouble competing with newer retail areas along other roads nearby. Strong population figures, tourist activity, and a lack of available vacant land for new development indicate strong redevelopment potential for the corridor.

In 2000, local government leaders along the 32-mile (52 km) route formed the State Road 7/U.S. 441 Collaborative. Now stretching to 41 miles (66 km), the collaborative is the longest revitalization effort in the country. The goal of the collaborative—which includes all 17 of the municipalities that SR-7 traverses and is supported by the South

Photos of existing conditions on State Road 7 show an automobile-dominated corridor with few amenities for transit riders. (STATE ROAD 7 COLLABORATIVE)

Florida Regional Planning Council—is to create a mixed-use, transit-oriented corridor with high-density activity centers located at primary intersections.

The collaborative has undertaken extensive planning and community outreach activities, funded in part by a $1.9 million grant from the U.S. Federal Highway Administration. A ULI Advisory Services panel visited the corridor in 2004 and suggested that nodal redevelopment take place at the highway's major and minor intersections, with less intensive redevelopment between those nodes. Community input, gathered through charrettes and interviews, revealed that citizens wanted redevelopment, improved public transit facilities and services, and new housing for all income levels, among other goals. "The charrette and the planning process set the stage," according to Gary Rogers, executive director of the Lauderdale Lakes Community Redevelopment Agency and vice chair of the SR-7 Collaborative.

A strategic master plan for Broward County was adopted in 2004, with multiple updates since then. That plan changed the land use designation along SR-7 to "transit-oriented corridor" and promoted smart growth principles. A right-of-way improvement plan specifies recommended streetscape improvements, and three-dimensional site plan regulations offer clear, concise descriptions. The hope is that with the appropriate infrastructure and regulatory framework in place, further redevelopment—including the addition of dense office, retail, and residential space—will occur.

Major infrastructure changes to be implemented include the widening of SR-7 to accommodate future transportation needs in some areas, as well as street-width

*Below left:* A rendering depicts plans to redesign the Greenway Canal in Lauderdale Lakes for recreational use. *Below:* A map shows the State Road 7 Collaborative area, which stretches 41 miles (66 km) and spans 17 municipalities. (STATE ROAD 7 COLLABORATIVE)

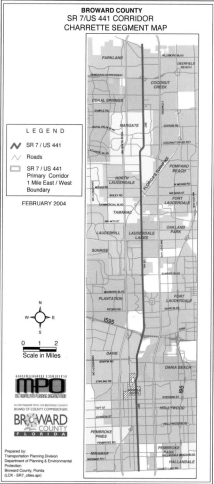

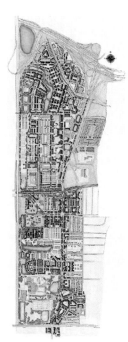
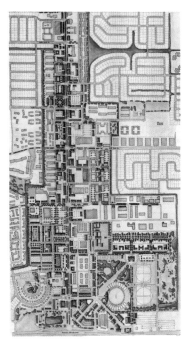

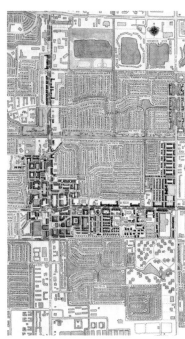

Municipalities in the State Road 7 Collaborative have created master plans to guide future development. (STATE ROAD 7 COLLABORATIVE)

reductions in others, to facilitate urban-scale redevelopment and accommodate premium transit (such as fixed rail or BRT). Pedestrian amenities, such as high-visibility crosswalks and medians to serve as crossing oases, will also be built. Necessary sewer infrastructure is being constructed.

Local transit service is currently provided throughout the corridor but is intended to evolve over time. Express service overlays are being introduced through pilot programs using bus queue jump lanes on SR-7. Eventually, a premium transit system in dedicated lanes will be established using bus or fixed-rail transit.

Improvements to bus stops along the corridor offer ample seating and shade. These photos show conditions before and after improvements. (STATE ROAD 7 COLLABORATIVE)

Lauderdale Lakes has replaced a number of obsolete bus shelters with 12 new open-air shelters that feature real-time arrival message displays, with another ten planned. A weed-filled, virtually abandoned corridor along a major regional drainage canal has been transformed into a two-mile-long (3.2 km) nonvehicular path that connects city government facilities, commercial centers, schools, and recreational facilities.

SR-7 corridor investments during the last ten years have totaled more than $165 million, including $137 million in right-of-way acquisition and construction, $10 million in transit enhancements, $10 million in sewer line infrastructure updates, and $4 million in bus shelter construction. Funding has been provided by the U.S. Department of Transportation, the state, regional planning bodies, and the John D. and Catherine T. MacArthur Foundation, as well as through local in-kind services and funding from local governments. The Florida Department of Transportation has made a financial commitment to supporting the state road, and the Broward County Metropolitan Planning Organization has committed to finding funds to build transit once the feasibility of light rail or BRT has been determined.

Redevelopment of the land along SR-7 has proved challenging, despite the adoption of new land use and zoning standards. Challenges include land assembly and the need to extend sewer infrastructure to places where it does not currently exist, with the economic downturn stalling development of the Lauderdale Lakes Town Center and other sites along the corridor. The work of reinventing SR-7 continues.

*Top and bottom:* Renderings show hoped-for improvements and development in Lauderdale Lakes, one of the State Road 7 Collaborative communities. *Below:* Charrettes and public meetings were essential to formulating plans for the transformation of State Road 7. (STATE ROAD 7 COLLABORATIVE)

# White Flint/Rockville Pike, Montgomery County, Maryland

*Rockville Pike in Montgomery County is relying heavily on the private sector for its transformation. Major property owners in the automobile-dominated corridor have come together to support a new sector plan, rally the public behind it, and fund the needed infrastructure investments.*

A rendering shows the future of the Pike and Rose project, one of several walkable, mixed-use projects being built at White Flint. (FEDERAL REALTY INVESTMENT TRUST)

### Lessons from White Flint/Rockville Pike

- Savvy property owners who recognize that transportation improvements allow for additional density and create value may be willing to tax themselves to pay for those investments.

- The private sector can help plan and fund infrastructure improvements that cash-strapped governments may be unable to do on their own.

Rockville Pike, a six-lane major arterial, runs through the northern suburbs of Washington, D.C., from the intensively developed inner-ring suburbs of Montgomery County into the less developed but still populous Frederick County. Much of Rockville Pike is paralleled underground by the heavy-rail Red Line, run by the Washington Metropolitan Area Transit Authority, although surface uses remain squarely auto dominated.

In Bethesda, Rockville Pike is home to the 43-acre (17.4 ha) White Flint Mall and is one of the highest income-generating areas in the county and state. However, the corridor is frequently congested, and the heavy traffic and orientation to drivers create safety and access issues for pedestrians, with surface parking lots standing between the road and buildings. Many Rockville Pike users are visitors to regional shopping centers and workers in office buildings, but pedestrian circulation is limited, and the few transit-

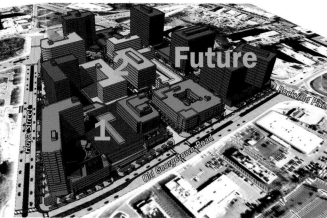

The phasing plan for the Pike and Rose project shows how density will be incrementally added by increasing height and constructing new streets.
(FEDERAL REALTY INVESTMENT TRUST)

oriented nodes around Red Line stations are not well connected to one another and other area land uses.

In recent years, developers in the corridor have been working with one another and other stakeholders to transform the area's land use and transportation patterns. The White Flint Partnership, formed in 2008 as a collaboration of the area's six major real estate players, has been working with local planning agencies and a transportation consultant to develop, implement, and fund a new vision for the area. The goal that has emerged from this work is a denser, mixed-use, walkable, and transit-friendly corridor.

The White Flint Sector Plan, completed in April 2010, lays out land uses in 430 acres (174 ha) along Rockville Pike. The current properties in the White Flint Sector are mostly zoned for commercial uses, and many acres are occupied by surface parking lots. The vision calls for almost 10,000 new housing units along this corridor and greater density of both residences and retail around the Metro station, in order to form an identifiable center. An extensive community outreach program—including a sustained social network–based outreach effort—helped gain public buy-in for the additional density and other recommendations.

The area's transportation infrastructure will also be transformed. The sector plan establishes a connection among land uses, transit, motorists, bicyclists, and pedestrians. It aims to transform Rockville Pike from a traffic-clogged roadway into a 21st-century boulevard with wide sidewalks, streetfront retail, dedicated bike lanes, and a center lane dedicated to BRT. An expanded, pedestrian-friendly road network with 16 new roads will put the entire area within a ten-minute walk of some form of public transportation. The more fine-grained street grid will help diffuse congestion and support a more mixed-use and less auto-dependent area.

Francine Waters, managing director of transportation/smart growth enterprises for Lerner Enterprises and executive director of the White Flint Partnership, described the role that property owners will play in funding the improvements. Because public funds for such projects are limited, landowners agreed to the creation of a special property tax district, as well as to pay for the construction of new roads and upgrades to existing roads on their properties. Why? Waters explains: "With public transportation, with the new network of streets, with the greater accessibility and more mobility, the value of the property rises incredibly. The members of the White Flint Partnership recognized that they are creating value."

The White Flint Development District was created to levy and collect an ad valorem property tax of ten cents per $100 of assessed value. Begun in July 2011, the tax will generate about $169 million for infrastructure improvements over 30 years. Developers will pay for an additional $280 million of improvements and the county will invest $152 million, for a total infrastructure development tab of approximately $601 million. The three-phase project is expected to create $1.3 billion in net new property revenue, $7 billion in new property tax revenue, and 39,000 new full-time jobs by 2030.

More recently, the partnership has expanded its vision beyond the immediate White Flint area to nearby federal installations, which the partnership hopes to connect with enhanced bus service. Extending the BRT to major federal health and science campuses could create a science and health triangle, adding vibrancy and enhancing potential revenues at White Flint.

*Above:* This rendering from the White Flint Sector Plan shows a transformed Rockville Pike, with multimodal transportation improvements and new bus rapid transit. (FEDERAL REALTY INVESTMENT TRUST) *Below:* The effort seeks to connect the 43-acre (17.4 ha) area with the larger region. (THE WHITE FLINT PARTNERSHIP)

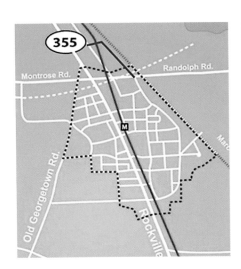

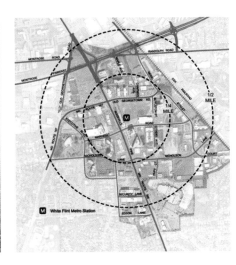

This rendering shows a denser, more human-scale environment at White Flint. (FEDERAL REALTY INVESTMENT TRUST)

Although plans are in place to fund and build transit-supportive infrastructure, significantly improved bus service in the corridor will depend on the success of a countywide effort to implement BRT service. This new system will also likely rely on property tax assessments for funding.

Reconstruction of Rockville Pike has not yet started, although new developments, including Federal Realty's Pike and Rose project, have recently broken ground. When complete, Rockville Pike will be transformed from an auto-oriented corridor to one that is better able to use its enviable location and connections to transit to grow in more dense and pedestrian-friendly ways.

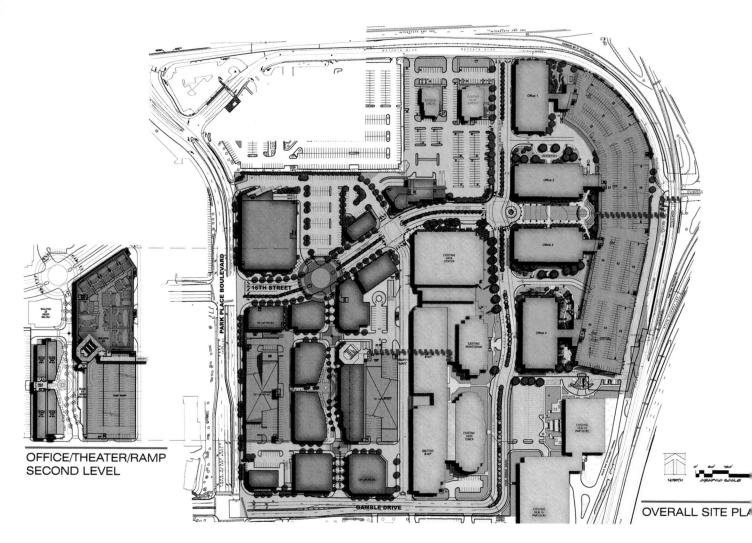

OFFICE/THEATER/RAMP
SECOND LEVEL

OVERALL SITE PLA

# West End, St. Louis Park, Minnesota

*The West End development, located in the suburbs of Minneapolis, is adding new retail, office, and housing offerings and making major infrastructure upgrades to create a new mixed-use lifestyle center for the region.*

The West End project, shown here in a site plan, repurposed a big-box site as a denser, more multiuse district. (DUKE REALTY)

## Lessons from the West End

- A lack of abutting residential uses can make redevelopment efforts easier.

- Multiple jurisdictions make entitlements more difficult and time-consuming. Ongoing collaboration is critical.

Located four miles (6.4 km) west of downtown Minneapolis, the West End infill development is set on a 32-acre (12.9 ha) site at the crux of two highways, Interstate 394 and State Highway 100. When Duke Realty began planning the development of the property in 2004, it contained two office towers, two freestanding restaurants, six low-rise office buildings, a data center, and another large, low-rise industrial structure. It straddled two suburban cities, with 26 acres (10.5 ha) in St. Louis Park and the other six acres (2.4 ha) in neighboring Golden Valley.

Duke Realty was interested in the site because, as Pat Mascia, senior vice president of Minneapolis–Saint Paul operations for the company, put it, "We had great demographics that would support a regional retail project," as well as "the best office development site in the Twin Cities. Putting retail and office uses together on this site created some great opportunities."

The city of St. Louis Park sought to connect the site to the city and make it a much denser, genuine, lasting place, one that was both pedestrian and transit friendly. The city of Golden Valley was also an important stakeholder. In 2008, Duke Realty broke ground on the project.

Today, the West End is a compact, pedestrian-oriented mixed-use project with 14 acres (5.7 ha) of office space, a 350,000-square-foot ( 32,516 m²) lifestyle retail center with 30,000 square feet (2,787 m²) of second-story office space, new entertainment offerings, and improved connections to existing office and shopping destinations in the area. A 119-unit apartment building broke ground in July 2012. Still to be built are 1.1 million square feet (102,193 m²) of office space in four towers.

Significant infrastructure investments—to provide improved connections between the new retail and existing office space—were needed. New roads were built and others widened; two parking structures were built to accommodate 1,500 stalls, and an additional 4,400-stall parking structure will be constructed to accompany the new office towers. Utility infrastructure (storm and sanitary sewers, water mains, gas lines,

Parking garages were pushed underground or to the perimeter of the site to enhance the walkable aspects of the West End project. These images show the site before and after redevelopment. (DUKE REALTY)

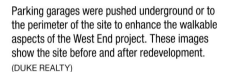

The West End project offers retail and restaurant activities throughout the day. (DUKE REALTY)

## Corridors of Opportunity Project Promotes Vibrant Communities

Corridors of Opportunity (CoO) is an initiative of the Metropolitan Council—the regional planning agency that serves the seven-county Minneapolis–Saint Paul metropolitan area—to promote sustainable, vibrant, and healthy communities by using the region's emerging transitway system as a development focus.

The initiative, which will run from 2011 to 2013, is funded by about $20 million that comes in the form of a Sustainable Communities Regional Planning Grant from the U.S. Department of Housing and Urban Development, as well as loans and grants from Living Cities, a collaborative of 22 of the nation's largest foundations and financial institutions.

A broad consortium of policy makers, foundations, community organizations, and local and regional leaders has joined the Metropolitan Council in this effort, and CoO's 21-member policy board meets regularly. The initiative's operating principles focus on equity, economic competitiveness, clarity, sustainability, collaboration, and innovation. Susan Haigh, chair of the Metropolitan Council and cochair of its CoO initiative, stressed, "What we're trying to do is align our planning efforts around our transit corridors to get a greater return on investment, to attract more private capital, and to make sure that we see these corridors of opportunity benefiting people of all incomes."

CoO is funding about two dozen discrete projects along seven existing and planned transitways, all of which are at different stages of planning or development: Southwest LRT, the Bottineau Corridor, the Gateway Corridor, Cedar Avenue Bus Rapid Transit, Central Corridor LRT, Hiawatha LRT, and Northstar Commuter Rail. The initiative is seeking the following improvements:

■ Better integration of multiple planning processes;

■ Greater participation from historically underrepresented groups;

and electrical and communications conduits) was carefully coordinated to keep the streetscape looking seamless. A below-ground water retention system, with drains to collect stormwater that is used to irrigate street trees and other plantings, won Duke Realty accolades in 2010 for decreasing pollutant runoff and improving water quality.

A new road—West End Boulevard—was designed as a winding, pedestrian-friendly promenade running through the property from east to west, with sidewalk cafés, street furniture, and green spaces. Kevin Teppen, senior landscape architect involved with the project, said, "It gives you that sense of place, that opportunity to stroll down the street, to gather and mill around." On the other hand, West 16th Street was not continued beyond the West End—partly because the city of Golden Valley wanted to protect nearby residential neighborhoods from traffic impacts—although other improvements were made.

The site is currently served by bus transit, and more intensive transit may be developed in the future. The project is also bike friendly; the city of St. Louis Park required parking for 35 bicycles on the site, and designers accommodated that requirement by placing bike racks on sidewalks and in parking garages.

The $400 million project received partial financing from the city of St. Louis Park, which created a tax increment financing district and contributed $21 million in TIF funds and $5 million to rebuild an existing road.

The site's location in two cities complicated entitlement, with two separate planning and approval processes required. Although Duke hoped to receive approvals quickly and begin construction by 2007, the process ended up taking more than three years. "And that was *fast* for us," said Kevin Locke, director of community development for the city of St. Louis Park. "We were able to fast-track this, partly because we didn't have any residential neighborhoods abutting it, which was a huge plus."

The delay wound up being a blessing for Duke. "We got our development agreement in December 2007 and started going vertical on the construction in April 2008," said Mascia. "The world fell off the cliff around October 2008." If construction had begun a year earlier, he noted, "we would have been opening the center right about the time the economy tanked. Instead, we hit the market at a time when some retailers were doing deals again." Duke focused on attracting retail tenants that were new to the Minneapolis–Saint Paul metro area, those that were opening their first or second store in the region and that fit well within the area's demographics.

Collaboration—among the developer, both cities, designers, and other stakeholders— was critical. "Over the course of many years of meeting weekly, we developed an outstanding relationship, which finally made this project happen," noted Mascia. With over 80 percent of current retail and office space already leased, the project is proving to be a successful first-ring suburb destination, and it has spurred other development in the area.

*Above:* Pedestrian-friendly features include street furniture and programmed open space. (DUKE REALTY)

*Facing page:* Using plazas and open space, events and outdoor concerts contribute to the West End's vibrancy. (DUKE REALTY)

For example, along the suburban Cedar Avenue BRT line, the initiative is striving to spur development in a suburban context. That three-component effort is looking at the existing market conditions at the station areas, identifying barriers that would prevent developers and lenders from working there, and creating a BRT station analysis that will become a guide for development activity along the corridor. The analysis involves creating a development typology, including preferred land uses, development practices, and funding opportunities tailored to BRT projects, coupled with a local engagement strategy along the corridor and efforts to promote interjurisdictional and interagency collaboration.

CoO is also working to accelerate the buildout of the transit system by looking at financial and political tools used by other transit systems. A related effort is being led by the Itasca Project, a business coalition that is estimating the return on investment of alternate transit buildout scenarios, including an accelerated one.

Moreover, the CoO initiative is making a significant investment—about $700,000—in grassroots community organizing that aims to build capacity in smaller organizations, to enable them to effectively influence transit and infrastructure decision making. And a $4.3 million CoO loan pool has been set up to help create and preserve affordable single- and multifamily housing in corridor neighborhoods.

The ultimate goal of the CoO initiative is to develop a new regional model for transitway development—as well as a regional plan for sustainable development—by aligning transit planning and engineering with land use planning, public and philanthropic investment, affordable housing, workforce development, and economic development.

# Richardson, Texas

*Richardson has sustained a two-decade commitment to transit-oriented development. Now home to significant TOD, Richardson is continuing to think about land use in the face of potential future transit expansion.*

## Lessons from Richardson

- A long-term commitment to TOD has helped Richardson leverage its transit asset. That work continues.

- Area residents—those living adjacent to a TOD project, as well as others—are important champions of projects, if they see the benefits.

Richardson, Texas, is a 28-square-mile (72.5 km²) suburban city, with about 102,500 residents and 120,000 jobs. Located ten miles (16.1 km) northeast of Dallas, the city—with four Dallas Area Rapid Transit (DART) stations on the Orange Line and a fifth planned along the as-yet-unbuilt Cotton Belt Line—has made a long-term commitment to working with DART on TOD.

Richardson's first major public/private partnership—developed by the Galatyn Park Corporation, DART, and the city—is the 27.5-acre (11.1 ha) Galatyn Park urban center, completed in 2002 to capitalize on the new Galatyn Park Station. The development includes a performing arts center, a public plaza, 283 apartments, 6,813 square feet (633 m²) of retail and restaurant space, and a 336-room hotel. Although several office buildings remain to be completed, the project has spurred additional development on adjacent land of a new Blue Cross/Blue Shield of Texas corporate headquarters complex.

Also nearby, the Nortel campus has seen recent development with Ericsson Inc. having more than doubled its footprint in 2011, and State Farm unveiling plans to expand into one of the largest office blocks on the campus in August 2012. Two transit-oriented developments, Amli Galatyn Station and Eastside, opened within a half mile (0.8 km) of the Galatyn Park Station in 2008 and 2009, providing high-end, mixed-use amenities for residents and visitors.

The Arapaho Center Station includes a pedestrian underpass and appealing landscaping to connect the transit center to surrounding mixed-use development. (DALLAS AREA RAPID TRANSIT)

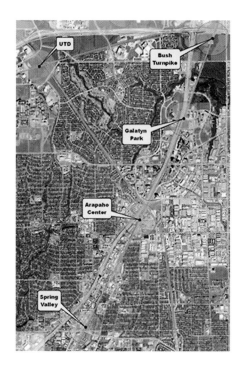

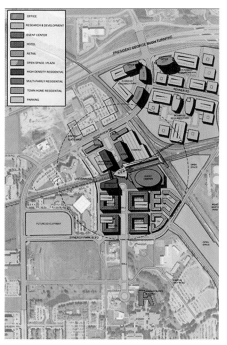

Following the success of Galatyn Park Station development, the area around Richardson's Arapaho Center Station was transformed into an adaptive use project with 14.8 acres (6.0 ha) of mixed-use development and a one-acre (0.4 ha) central park that opened in 2007. The Spring Valley Station experienced the addition of the Brick Row TOD project that opened in 2008, bringing 500 apartments, 80,000 square feet (7,432 m²) of retail and restaurants, 140 townhouses, 300 condominiums, and 11,000 square feet (1,022 m²) of office space to the area around the station.

Near the fourth and final existing station, Bush Turnpike Station, a 220-acre (89 ha) parcel is in the planning stages to become a new transit-oriented development led by the Parliament Group. This project will be part of a projected $1.5 billion mixed-use development on 300 acres (121 ha) along George Bush Turnpike and US-75. To

The Brick Row Urban Village takes advantage of its proximity to the Spring Valley DART station. (BRICK ROW URBAN VILLAGE)

## Dallas Area Rapid Transit: TOD Innovator

Although it has been in existence only since 1983, Dallas Area Rapid Transit (DART) now operates the longest light-rail transit (LRT) system in the United States, with 77 miles (124 km) of track and 58 stations serving about 700 square miles (1,813 km²). Another 22 miles (35 km) and nine stations are planned by 2019, including an extension to Dallas–Fort Worth International Airport, as well as more than 12,000 bus stops. From the beginning, DART has viewed fostering transit-oriented development around its stations as part of its mission. DART's mission has included improving the quality of life and stimulating development within its service area; partnering with its 13 member cities to encourage TOD is a natural outcome of that mission. Recent efforts have included the development of a new rating system to evaluate TOD potential and establish priorities.

The Dallas metro area's ambitious buildout of the light-rail system has been funded by a 1983 sales tax ballot measure. David Leininger, chief financial officer at DART, noted that future funding solutions will be more complex, consisting of a blend of value capture; innovative financing, including naming rights and sponsorships; fares; and taxes. TOD—with its ability to enhance revenues from many of those sources—is an important part of DART's overall financial picture.

Diverse TOD projects have been completed along DART's lines; types include urban and suburban infill, suburban greenfield, and adaptive use projects. Estimates for 2009 indicated that over $8 billion of existing, in progress, and planned TOD projects were occurring along DART corridors. Almost $100 million of state and local tax revenue will be generated over the construction period of the DART buildout alone, with $4 billion in

facilitate this development, the city recently initiated new TOD zoning around the station, which will eventually connect with the Cotton Belt Line. A TIF district has been created to help fund the continuing development of the area, and the city has streamlined its development approval process.

A 2000 ULI Advisory Services panel helped set the stage for TOD in Richardson. The study "was quite useful in terms of getting developers and landowners around the table to start talking about TOD and mixed-use development," noted Gary Slagel, mayor of the city from 1991 to May 2011. Slagel is currently a member of DART's board of directors.

Looking forward, Richardson is undertaking a station area master plan for a future Dallas Cotton Belt station, which is a joint project of the city of Richardson and the

University of Texas at Dallas. The proposed station would connect the university to Dallas–Fort Worth Airport and would serve as the focal point for a new walkable, mixed-use development, including residential, retail, office, and research and development facilities; an event center; a hotel; and public open spaces.

Because developing mixed-use projects near neighborhoods of single-family homes is challenging, Richardson has worked to communicate regularly with residents and to persuade them of transit-oriented development's benefits. "Involve, involve, involve," Slagel urged—and not just those who live adjacent to a new project, but the entire city.

Richardson's early and aggressive pursuit of transit-oriented development has helped the city emerge as a TOD model and success story. The city has realized significant increases in property values at each of the four completed DART stations.

regional economic activity over a five-year period resulting in thousands of new jobs.

Jack Wierzenski, director of economic development for DART, explained, "Our philosophy for TOD is to work with the development community and with our member cities, thinking outside the box." DART encourages development that is tailored to each specific site, relying on partnerships with member cities, other government entities, and the private sector.

In August 2008, DART adopted a formal TOD policy that calls for the agency to work in close partnership with its member cities to identify and implement TOD opportunities. By promoting high-quality TOD, the agency is creating revenue for DART, as well as fostering environmentally sustainable, livable communities focused on transit accessibility. The 13 member cities are important partners, since they have the financial tools—like TIF, public improvement districts, and grants—and the land use authority needed to make infrastructure improvements and to leverage TOD projects.

In 2009, DART took advantage of the stagnant economy to step back, look at the properties it owned, and create a new TOD evaluation and prioritization system. It developed four evaluation criteria—property attributes, accessibility, third-party interest, and market potential—that it broke down into a point system. The 20 top-ranked properties are now TOD priority areas for the agency. Moving forward, DART is reevaluating the rankings and adjusting them as appropriate. "This has been very successful," Wierzenski commented, "not only to get ourselves at DART focused, but to get our member cities focused on where DART is moving with their properties in the future."

*Facing page, top:* New development is located close to the DART rail line. *Bottom:* The Eisemann Center at Galatyn Park has become a cultural destination for the Dallas metro area. (DALLAS AREA RAPID TRANSIT)

# CityCentre, Houston, Texas

*A mixed-use development built on the site of a former mall, west Houston's 37-acre (15 ha) CityCentre project is a pedestrian-friendly, mixed-use destination with a one-acre (0.4 ha) heavily programmed plaza at its center.*

The focal point of CityCentre is a meticulously designed and heavily programmed plaza.
(CITYCENTRE)

### Lessons from CityCentre

■ Employers care about where their employees will shop, eat, and live. Office tenants can be enticed by retail and restaurant offerings and residential opportunities.

■ Effectively programmed and managed spaces are powerful attractors of people—and dollars.

■ Retention of existing structured parking facilities saved tens of millions of dollars in development costs.

The CityCentre project, which opened in spring 2010, was built on the site of an obsolete mall in the suburbs of Houston, Texas. The project's developer, Midway, has transformed the site into a thriving destination, with office, residential, and entertainment offerings. CityCentre's complex includes 400,000 square feet (37,161 m²) of retail and entertainment space, 425,000 square feet (39,484 m²) of office space, and 149,000 square feet (13,843 m²) of fitness facilities. The development has 700 residential units ranging from brownstones to lofts, a 255-room luxury hotel topped with six condominiums, and a movie theater. With the recent addition of three office buildings, the project is complete.

CityCentre, located along a major highway in Houston, replaced an outmoded mall with over 1 million square feet (93,000 m²) of mixed-use development. (CITYCENTRE)

Midway purchased the site because of its location at the demographic center of Houston. Located at the intersection of Beltway 8 and I-10, 2 million people live within a 20-minute drive of the property. Beltway 8 is the middle of three beltways that will eventually ring the city. Because the city of Houston is so vast (with a total land area of 579 square miles [1,500 km²]), much suburban-style development is located within city boundaries.

Three parking structures on the property, built for the old mall and retained in the CityCentre project, can accommodate 11,500 daily visitors in approximately 4,000 spaces, and CityCentre is visible to nearly 500,000 cars per day. But developer Midway

CityCentre features carefully crafted design elements and landscaping. (CITYCENTRE)

emphasized pedestrian circulation within the site. New, narrow streets built within the project and on-street parking add to an urban, compact feel.

The mixed-use nature of the development can create powerful linkages, said Jonathan Brinsden, chief operating officer and executive vice president of Midway. "From an investment standpoint," he noted, "there can be tremendous synergies and value creation, if all the pieces truly add to each other. The risk is that if you get one piece wrong, it can affect the other pieces negatively." He cited CityCentre's appealing retail, fitness, entertainment, and restaurant offerings as powerful drivers of office and residential rents; CityCentre brings in some of the highest office and residential rents in the city, and its hotel has the third-highest revenue per available room in Houston.

Noting that "with the two big demographic bubbles, almost all of our residents are either empty nesters or new young professionals," Brinsden added that his team focused on providing the types of amenities and experiences those households want, like a fitness center and spa, cinema restaurant, and motor club.

Midway has also emphasized place management, including programming in the plaza, which has been key to attracting shoppers and others night after night. "The town square is still in our DNA; it's part of who we are," Brinsden noted. Events in CityCentre's plaza—more than 150 per year—help build relationships with workers, residents, and visitors.

CityCentre's compact form and pedestrian emphasis set it apart from other developments in Houston. But ironically, the development was easy to entitle— Houston's lack of a zoning code means that planning and developing a site like CityCentre are much simpler than they might be in other municipalities.

# Contributors

All opinions, errors, and omissions are our own. The views expressed in this report do not necessarily reflect those of individual ULI members.

The ULI Infrastructure Initiative gratefully acknowledges the contributions of the following people:

**Heather Alhadeff**
Senior Transportation Planner
Perkins + Will
Atlanta, Georgia

**Ranadip Bose**
Senior Project Manager
SB Friedman & Company
Chicago, Illinois

**Jonathan Brinsden**
Executive Vice President and Chief
  Operating Officer
Midway
Houston, Texas

**Colleen Carey**
President
The Cornerstone Group
Richfield, Minnesota

**Scott Condra**
Senior Vice President
Jacoby Development Inc.
Atlanta, Georgia

**Caren Dewar**
Executive Director
ULI Minnesota
Minneapolis, Minnesota

**Larry Dorr**
Director of Finance and City Treasurer
City of Lakewood
Lakewood, Colorado

**Jeff Dufresne**
Executive Director
ULI Atlanta
Atlanta, Georgia

**Jim Durrett**
Executive Director, Buckhead Community
  Improvement District
Chair, MARTA
Atlanta, Georgia

**Dan Eernissee**
Economic Development Program
  Manager
City of Shoreline
Shoreline, Washington

**Terry Foegler**
Director of Strategic Initiatives
City of Dublin
Dublin, Ohio

**Susan Haigh**
Chair
Metropolitan Council
Saint Paul, Minnesota

**John Heagy**
Vice President
Hines
Atlanta, Georgia

**Jason Jordan**
Director
Center for Transportation Excellence
Washington, D.C.

**Bonnie Kollodge**
Public Relations Senior Manager
Metropolitan Council
Saint Paul, Minnesota

**David Leininger**
Chief Financial Officer
Dallas Area Rapid Transit
Dallas, Texas

**Tad Leithead**
Chair
Atlanta Regional Commission
Atlanta, Georgia

**Jay Lindgren**
Partner
Dorsey & Whitney LLP
Minneapolis, Minnesota

**Kevin Locke**
Executive Director, St. Louis Park Housing
  Authority
Director, Community Development
  Department
St. Louis Park, Minnesota

**Donna Adams Mahaffey**
Chief of External Affairs
Perimeter Community Improvement
  Districts
Dunwoody, Georgia

**Neil Marciniak**
Economic Development Specialist
City of Lakewood
Lakewood, Colorado

**Pat Mascia**
Senior Vice President of Minneapolis–
  Saint Paul Operations
Duke Realty
Minneapolis, Minnesota

**Helen McCarthy**
Senior Communications Specialist
Duke Realty
Minneapolis, Minnesota

**Kirk McKinley**
Transportation Services Manager, Public
  Works
City of Shoreline
Shoreline, Washington

**Ceasar Mitchell**
President
Atlanta City Council
Atlanta, Georgia

**Tom Murphy**
Joseph C. Canizaro/Klingbeil
  Family Chair
Urban Land Institute
Washington, D.C.

**Kathleen Osher**
Executive Director
Transit Alliance
Denver, Colorado

**Patrick Phillips**
Chief Executive Officer
Urban Land Institute
Washington, D.C.

**Kenneth Powell**
Managing Director, Public Finance
Stone & Youngberg LLC
Richmond, Virginia

**Dan Reuter**
Land Use Division Chief
Atlanta Regional Commission
Atlanta, Georgia

**Paul Rice**
Principal Planner
City of Lakewood
Lakewood, Colorado

**Gary Rogers**
Executive Director
Lauderdale Lakes Community
  Redevelopment Agency
Lauderdale Lakes, Florida

**Gary Slagel**
President and CEO
CapitalSoft Inc.
Former Mayor of Richardson
Richardson, Texas

**Lynnette Slater Crandall**
Partner
Dorsey & Whitney LLP
Minneapolis, Minnesota

**John Robert Smith**
President and CEO, Reconnecting
  America
Former Mayor, Meridian, Mississippi
Washington, D.C.

**Dave Stockert**
President and CEO
Post Properties Inc.
Atlanta, Georgia

**Jim Stokes**
Interim Executive Director
Livable Communities Coalition of Metro
  Atlanta
Atlanta, Georgia

**Eric Swanson**
Regional Planner/Policy Analyst
South Florida Regional Planning Council
Hollywood, Florida

**Tavia Tan**
Communications Assistant
City of Shoreline
Shoreline, Washington

**Kevin Teppen**
Senior Landscape Architect
McCombs Frank Roos Associates
Minneapolis, Minnesota

**Francine Waters**
Managing Director
Lerner Enterprises
Rockville, Maryland

**Jack Wierzenski**
Director of Economic Development
Dallas Area Rapid Transit
Dallas, Texas

**Monte Wilson**
Principal, Global Buildings
Jacobs
Atlanta, Georgia

**David Winstead**
Attorney
Ballard Spahr LLP
Washington, D.C.